Inspiring Stories of Love and Wisdom at the End of Life

Enduring Love

Hospice Portraits by *Mary Landberg*, RN

Mary Landberg

White Cloud Press
Ashland, Oregon

White Cloud Press books may be purchased for educational, business, or sales promotional use. For information,
please write: Special Market Department, White Cloud Press, PO Box 3400, Ashland, OR 97520
Website: www.whitecloudpress.com

Cover and Interior Design by C Book Services

First edition: 2014

Printed in the United States of America

14 15 16 17 18   10 9 8 7 6 5 4 3 2 1

Library of Congress Cataloging-in-Publication Data

Landberg, Mary.
Enduring love : inspiring stories of love and wisdom at the end of life / by Mary Landberg. -- First edition.
pages cm. -- (The humankind project)
Includes bibliographical references and index.
ISBN 978-1-940468-06-8 (paperback)
1. Terminally ill--Portraits. 2. Terminally ill--Family relationships. I. Title.
TR681.T47L36 2014
779'.9616029--dc23
2014012245

Enduring Love

Enduring Love is dedicated to all hospice workers, a compassionate and resilient group of dedicated people who offer one last act of kindness over and over again.

Introduction

Everybody dies. Some die suddenly and some pass away slowly. Rich and poor alike die the same way. Death is a great equalizer in this respect. Young and old from all walks of life and cultures die from cancer, heart disease, Alzheimer's, organ failure, and strokes. People die in nursing homes, 5th wheels, hospitals, track homes, mansions, and trailers.

The great similarity in the dying process regardless of economic status, age, or any cause or place of death is the way people lovingly touch each other. During this time of transition, there is little room for what is not true. For most, in the end love is all that is left; loving connection becomes all that matters. Love survives beyond the last breath. This enduring love is what I strive to photograph.

Hand portraiture preserves this significant expression of loving connection. Each hand is different, a symbol of identity that embodies character. Scars, age spots, calluses, and wrinkles tell stories of lives lived. Hands reveal honest emotion.

The testimonies I have received validate this important work. When a patient's wife tearfully told me that her hand portrait with her husband (on the last day of his life) was her most cherished object, 1 knew 1 had to keep doing this. At the time of this writing I have photographed over three hundred hospice patients and families.

I offer hospice portraiture free of charge. 1 gift family members with high-resolution images on a CD and a print or two. I do accept donations, which don't quite cover my costs of printing, framing, CDs, mailing supplies, and postage. It's a way I give back to my community; it feels good.

What sets *Enduring Love* apart from other hospice photography books is that the primary focus is not on the faces of hospice patients, but on their hands. The mystery of who belongs to the hands allows the hands to belong to anyone in the reader's life, perhaps offering a sense of comfort or completion.

Along with taking photographs, I have been participating in deeply meaningful conversations with the dying and their families. I've recorded their inspiring stories of wisdom, love, and history. I have selected over one hundred of their touching photographs and beautiful stories, along with my observations and insights, to include in this book.

All of my patients have been told they have six months or less to live. Along with that news comes a whirlwind of opportunities for me to help them to live and love while they are alive. I have witnessed and wholeheartedly believe that healing is possible while dying.

I am offered daily wake-up calls to the temporary nature of life. I have learned how to live by spending time with the dying. I want to share my experiences with you.

While reading *Enduring Love*, I hope you will gain a better understanding of the common fears about death and what physically and emotionally happens during the dying process. You will learn about the common struggles and resolve families and loved ones experience at the end of life. You will see how true love shows up in the world. You will see ways to initiate those difficult yet important conversations about death and dying. Most important, it is my sincere desire that you accept the invitation that *Enduring Love* offers to live and love fully while you are alive.

Please visit www.enduringlovebook.com

Enduring Love

Dennis didn't know it in this moment, but this was his last
"I love you."

This process of transition is a time when the living and dying are forced out of comfort zones and into the mystery of the end of life.

Loving touch. This is the last comfort. This is all that is left in the end.

Alzheimer's robbed Julia from sweet Orval, her devoted husband of sixty-two years. Yet he fed her lunch every day at the nursing home in hopes of a rare but promising glimpse of recognition. Every day she squirmed in suspicion of this stranger offering her a spoon full of puréed food. Julia consistently pushed his hand away. Sometimes she smacked him in the face. But his love was stronger than her fist. His unwavering love paid off on the day of this photograph. She allowed him to take her hand. He had tears in his eyes and said, "This is my Christmas."

Medford was thrilled with the idea of being photographed playing his piano, as he hadn't "performed" in decades. He even took his oxygen tubing off for the event (which he later pretended not to regret).

He knew for certain that he made it to ninety-four by playing his piano three hours every day for the last eighty years. His baby grand took up most of the living room of his tiny apartment. This is where he was most alive.

His dying wish was to ask world-renowned opera singer Renée Fleming some very specific questions about her "brilliant techniques." I took a chance and sent Renée an email with his detailed questions. I included this photo of Medford in my correspondence.

One week later Medford collapsed in his apartment. He had to be placed in a nursing home that afternoon, as his heart disease then rendered him completely dependent on others.

When I came home from that long day in hospice care, I found Renée's heartfelt email waiting. She apologized for the delay in responding. She was in London rehearsing for her next performance. I immediately called the nursing home and had Medford's niece hold the phone to his ear. As I read Renée's tender email to him, I heard him chuckle and sigh. He got his wish. Medford died six hours later.

Margaret's primary concern was to find a home for her beloved golden retriever, Bonnie. Margaret's cancer pain and impending death were secondary.

The love that these two souls shared was extraordinary. Bonnie's whole body wagged when Margaret walked in the front door. Margaret's smile quickly migrated from ear to ear when Bonnie offered her unconditional love and simple presence.

Their love for each other rivaled most human love.

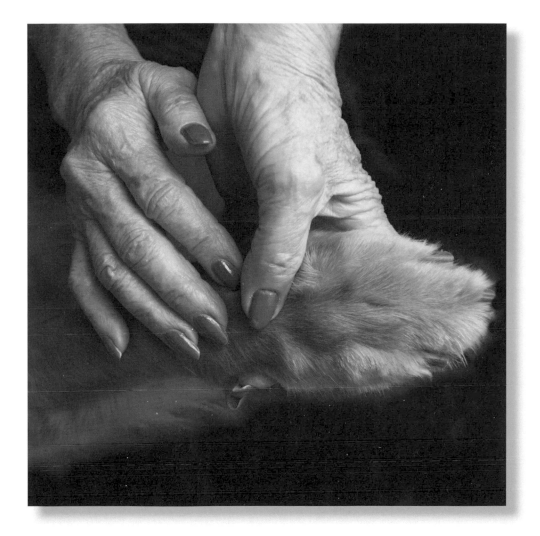

Gerry's stroke left her without speech or facial expression. She did have minimal use of her right arm and hand, however. It took about ten slow minutes, but Gerry's thumb inched its way up the bedrail until it made contact with her son's hand. Her son knew what she was trying to communicate by this simple, familiar, yet powerful connection.

I have spent hours alone with stroke victims thought to be incoherent. It must be terrifying to appear emotionless when you have thoughts and feelings to express. You and I communicate with body language, facial expression, and speech. Given the opportunity, some stroke victims left paralyzed and speechless can communicate quite well. A blink of an eye or tap of a finger can speak volumes.

Valerie was a feisty cocktail waitress at a honky-tonk. Bruce was a shy trucker who stopped in for a beer after a long haul. On the first evening she waited on him, he left her a $100 tip and a dinner invitation. She thanked him for the tip, but refused his company for dinner. "He wasn't my type," Valerie said to me. "He was too nice." Bruce was sweetly persistent; he regularly sent her flowers and kept up the big tips every week—for five long years. She finally said yes to a steak dinner. They married after six months of dating. Valerie regrets not having said yes to him sooner. "I had no idea he *was* my type." Bruce was diagnosed with early-onset Alzheimer's disease in his mid fifties and died at the age of sixty. They had fifteen amazing years together.

Examine what your "type" really is. Some hold out for an "ideal type," someone with certain physical features, income, or possessions. Maybe your type isn't what you think it is. Your type may be hidden in a package you would not expect.

Hands are for holding.

Early one morning in 1930, when Carl was fourteen, he left his mother a note before jumping on his horse and riding out West to realize his dream of being a cowboy.

> *Dear Ma, I'm going to Montana.*
> *I have the money I got for Christmas.*
> *My books are under Aunt's porch.*
> *I know I will make good.*
> *I prayed all last night I would.*
> *Please don't try to get me.*
> *With love to all, Carl*

He took a leap of faith that paid off. He became a successful rancher and found Wilma, the cowgirl of his dreams (although not in Montana, but in Texas). He hadn't wanted his mother to know his actual destination, because he knew she would jump on a horse and come look for him.

The original handwritten note to his mother is framed and hangs proudly above his bed at the assisted living facility where he now lives. Carl points it out to everyone who comes to visit to remind us all that dreams really can come true.

Nancy stroked his hand as he slowly slipped away. Between discreet sobs, she said he was a courageous man with an incredible will to live. I asked her to tell me about his courage. After a seemingly difficult silence, she told me he was a Bataan Death March survivor. I couldn't think of any more questions to ask.

Joy's appetite had been poor for months. She was losing weight and became too weak to walk anymore. All she wanted to do was stay in her room, hide under her covers, eat Ritz crackers, and watch Jeopardy DVDs. She had been bedbound for two weeks when I met her.

Since Joy was very hard of hearing, I leaned in close. Before I could finish, "Good morning Joy, how are you?", her granddaughter literally ripped my nametag off of my shirt. Her hands frantically waved over her head as she shouted in a whisper, "I don't want my grandmother to know that she is on hospice!"

Joy was 102.

Why do people fear death so much that they can't talk about it?

Robert and Patricia met in a movie theater in 1948. "She was with a different fellow," Robert boasted with a boyish smile. On that evening Robert convinced Patricia's date to allow him to walk her home. Patricia then loaned her bicycle to Robert to ride back to his home, six miles away. Of course they had to meet the next day so Robert could return her bike. From that day forward, "We held hands as much as possible," said Patricia, grinning and looking deep into Robert's eyes.

They gazed at each other with such delight and touched each other with an exquisite tenderness.

Johanna hid five small diamonds in a jar of cold cream before boarding the ship. She knew if they were discovered she would be executed on the spot. She had to take the risk for what was left of her family.

Johanna was a brave and courageous survivor of insurmountable odds back in the 1940s. As a petite young mother with fierce determination, she fled the inhumanity of her country and landed in the safety of the United States to start a new life for her family.

For one hundred and two years she had to stay strong. An unfamiliar softness surfaced the weeks prior to her passing. Her son said that she returned to her innocence, sweet simplicity, trusting and open.

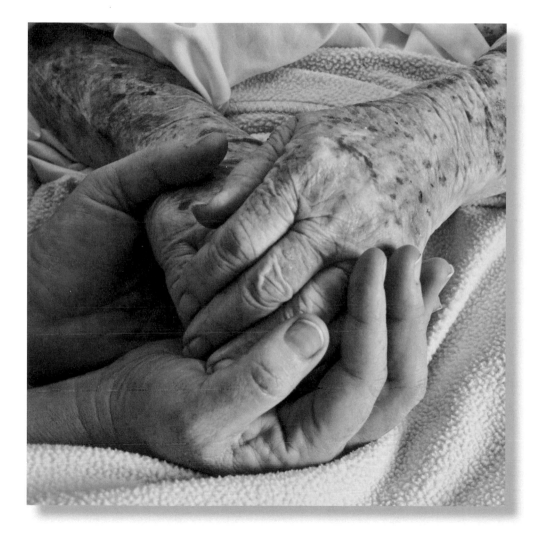

Great, GREAT Grandpa

For four months her grandfather lived in a hospital bed in her dining room where the dining table used to be. The dining chairs surrounded his bed. The family met for meals, with their grandfather happily in the center of conversation.

The dying often see their deceased parents and tell them with elation they are on their way. At this point, they are typically in a semi-conscious state within a week or two of passing. It is beautiful to witness the dying sharing their joyous visions of angels and all sorts of spiritual and religious figures commonly hovering up in the corners of their rooms. Calm words are spoken of packing, bringing the car around, and going home. Some get ready to hop on the train they hear coming, or rush people along so they don't miss the bus. I've been told that the suitcases are at the door and to be sure not to forget the big blue one with the presents in it.

At this time in the dying process, most hospice patients will be found reaching their arms up into the stillness above their bodies. When this happens, I slip my hand in theirs, and a lovely contentment can follow. I wonder whose hand they are reaching for, whose hand they think they are holding. It delights me to think that my hand could be representing the hand of God, their mother, their father, or their deceased child. Maybe their contentment comes from simply knowing that they are not alone.

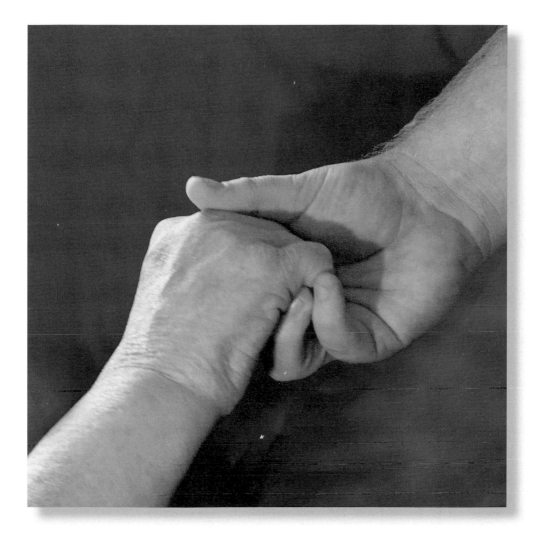

Helen always put her husband Don's needs first. He was living with moderate dementia; she was his primary caregiver in their home.

When Helen was diagnosed with pancreatic cancer, she immediately put their family home up for sale and moved her and Don into a locked dementia unit so that when she died, he would be safe.

Helen wanted to live with Don in the dementia unit so he could become familiar with the new environment, with her in it. It was also Helen's hope that by living there together, Don would be less afraid when she died.

Helen was sharp as a tack, but everyone she lived with had dementia and needed twenty-four-hour supervision and care. I don't know if I could do it, but Helen felt as though it was not only an honor to do so, but also her heartfelt choice. She said with certainty that Don would do the same for her if he could.

In my mind, Helen was a hero. She lived in that locked unit in beautiful respect for the residents about six months. She took a mother hen role for many. She said her strong faith in God pulled her through. Her unwavering commitment to her beloved husband left him safe and unafraid when she died.

At eighty-three, Van was the newest resident and most eligible bachelor in the retirement community. His son Rich said, "He was a gentleman with a sweet disposition and a consistent, kind nature." That news spread fast. All the elderly single ladies made their attempts to get Van's attention, except for one. Lois didn't need to bat her eyes; she and Van found each other instantly at a bridge social. They soon wed in style and spent over a decade living life fuller than most half their age. Their stories of world travel and taking risks for fun were impressive. Van was known as someone who would try anything once, from roller blading in Malibu at eighty-four to riding elephants in Thailand at ninety.

Van and Lois had lived entire lifetimes before starting their new life together. Could you and I increase our odds of another go at love and adventure in our mid eighties? Yes! Many people reach retirement age and start suffering the consequences of living stressful lives with unhealthy routines. Believe me, I see it daily.

Find ways to be kinder to yourself and others. It's never too late to start. Investing in yourself now could pay off in big adventure in your future.

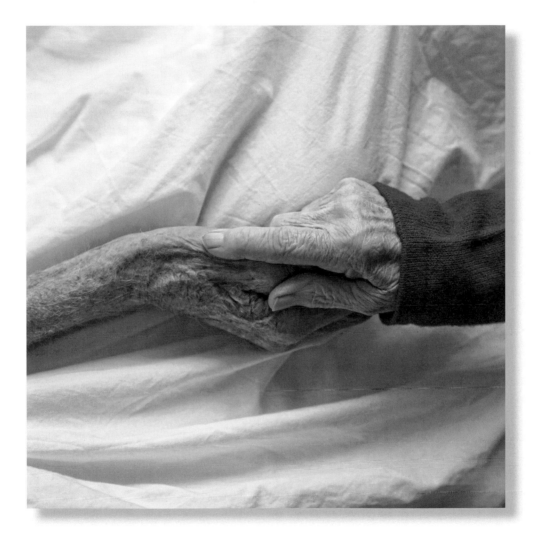

His little sister died about two weeks after this photograph was taken. He loved her with a certainty that he will see her again someday. It is my hope that this photograph will keep that memory alive.

Leetha literally knit miles of warm scarves and baby blankets for families she would never meet. She founded the "Fairy Godmothers," a dynamic trio of spry eighty-something gals who knit for the needy. She also volunteered decades of her time to alterations and clothing repairs for the residents of the assisted living facility where she lived. She knit and sewed well into the last week of her life.

Leetha's busy hands finally get to rest.

Ralph became restless at the end of every meal because he found himself without money to pay his bill. At eighty-eight with moderate dementia, he couldn't grasp the idea that all of his meals were included in the price of his room and board at the care facility. Janice, his caregiver, gave him an expired credit card to put in his wallet. Every night thereafter he would buy everyone's dinner and drinks. "Just put in on the card!" he would broadcast with delight while waving the credit card over his head.

Another resident, Margaret, had been a long-time smoker and was mourning the loss of her calming routine of having a cigarette after dinner. Janice bought a pack of her favorite brand, destroyed the actual cigarettes, and replaced them with rolled paper. She colored on red tips and brown filters. Margaret's after-dinner joy was back.

Janice's creative genius finds ways of calming her residents who suffer from Sundowners Syndrome or the general agitation that can accompany dementia. Many caregivers take the easier route of medicating the agitated. Janice gives hugs and kisses as a first step of care, then offers distraction, assesses for pain, hunger, thirst, and toileting needs. Agitation can be a symptom of many things, especially the loss of independence and the familiar.

Lee proudly said, "When I met Kenny he was a redneck cowboy, and I turned him into a biker dude."

Lee at five foot three and Kenny at six foot seven rode 365,442 miles over the course of their beautiful relationship and wore out three Harleys in the process. Before every ride they would kiss their own thumbs and rub them together for luck and as a promise of eternal love should they crash.

"He was my bodyguard and my hero. Thank you Kenny for the great journey we've been on together."

~Lee

Verla couldn't eat the chicken soup her daughter Darlene made from scratch; she choked with each weak attempt at swallowing. So Darlene drew up the broth in a syringe (meant for pain medication) and dripped it into her dying mother's mouth one drop at a time. As I walked in, I heard an exasperated Darlene say, "I love you, Mom. Eat!" Verla was in her last two weeks of life.

As we grow up, most of us learn to nurture with food. We show affection for the people we care about via the kitchen. This is the only way some people know how to express love. When the dying no longer can accept food or water, some family members/caregivers find themselves at a loss.

When the dying body no longer requires food or water, the senses of hunger and thirst disappear. There is a blessing to dehydration. It promotes a deep sleep and eventual coma; this is not uncomfortable.

If we force food and water, the dying body doesn't know what to do with it. Food can sit in the gut and cause cramping, nausea, or vomiting. Unwanted fluid can also find its way into the lungs and cause a host of uncomfortable complications.

I suggest we offer food and water. If the dying are willing and able to accept it, keep offering. If they don't want it or choke, stop offering. Sometimes it's the most loving thing we can do.

Those who crossed Smitty's path fell in love with him. He was genuinely happy and had a presence about him that was rare for someone with advanced dementia.

On the day of this photograph, Smitty had been uncharacteristically anxious, probably because he was too weak to wheel himself around the care facility anymore. His devoted family arrived, surrounded him, and laid their hands on him. This spontaneous photograph tells of the sweet power of simple loving touch.

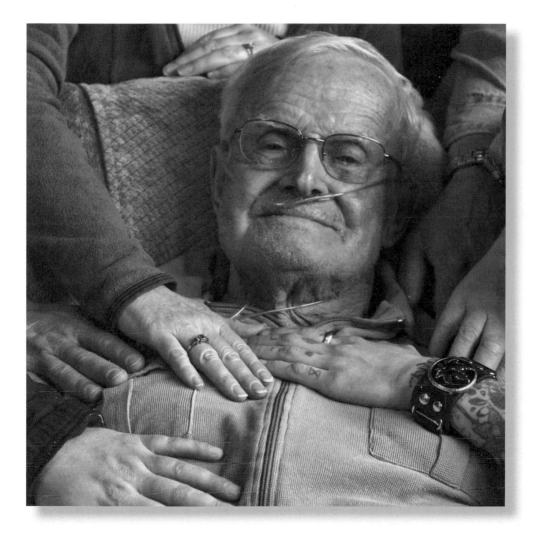

Heaven gained some awesome angels this year.

If the right moment presents itself, I ask hospice patients if they have any regrets about their lives. When I asked John this question, he said with pride, "I have fulfilled this life's purpose." Beaming he said, "I have had a successful life because I have been a loving, devoted husband for fifty-five years and a very proud father, grandfather, and great-grandfather."

Many people describe success in terms of accumulation of things and money in the bank. The happiest, most content people I've met describe success the way John did.

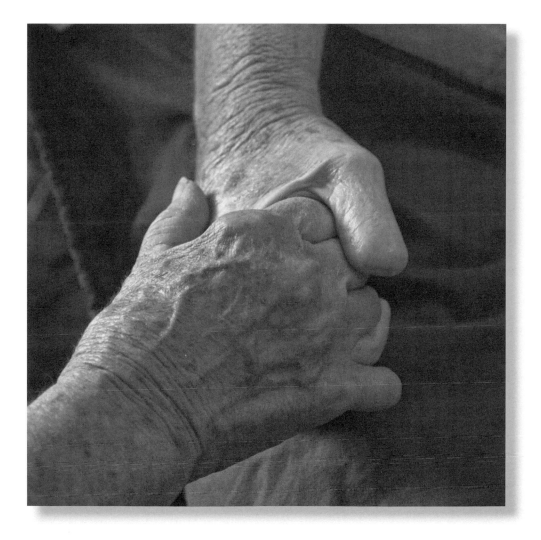

Tom was a salesman for Kodak, and in late summer 1940 he called on a dealer in Pasadena, California. Tom was told with a wink that there was a cute gal named Beth in the basement darkroom who needed help making enlargements. That same evening, after dining and dancing with her at the Biltmore Bowl, Tom proposed marriage. Beth rushed home to ask her mother's permission to marry Tom. Beth told me, "I was barely twenty years old, and I was betrothed to someone else!" That first whirlwind date was seventy-seven years ago.

I frequently ask couples if they have any advice for a long marriage. Tom quickly replied to my question with, "When you see something good, grab it! Don't wait for something better to come along." Beth said, "Tom cured me of a quick temper I inherited from my father." The first time Beth's special inheritance reared itself, Tom picked her up and put her in a cold shower fully clothed. He went into the shower with her, ruining his brand new cream herringbone suit in the process. They both laughed until they cried. They vowed "never to go to bed angry and to kiss a lot." With a daily good morning kiss, a welcome home kiss, and a goodnight kiss, Beth and I calculated that they had kissed a minimum of 84,855 times since they first met.

Geraldine was admitted to hospice because her primary care doctor thought that given her condition she probably wouldn't be alive in six months. This is the criteria for admission to hospice. Geraldine had lost quite a bit of weight over three months, was falling a few times a week, and was resistant to care between deep three-hour naps.

It turned out she was resistant to care because she was in pain. She fell because she got dizzy from low blood pressure when she stood up. Geraldine was sleepy because the medicine to calm her was sedating her. She wasn't alert enough to eat.

Sometimes we find elderly people managed by several doctors, all prescribing medications—too many medications. Or the elderly can't handle the dosage anymore. Aging kidneys and livers don't process medications as effectively, and medication levels can build in the blood and cause problems.

We medicated her pain, reduced her blood pressure medication, and completely eliminated her sedative. Within six weeks Geraldine was eating all of her meals, walking independently with a walker, and a joy to be around. Geraldine graduated from our service. Not everybody dies when admitted to hospice.

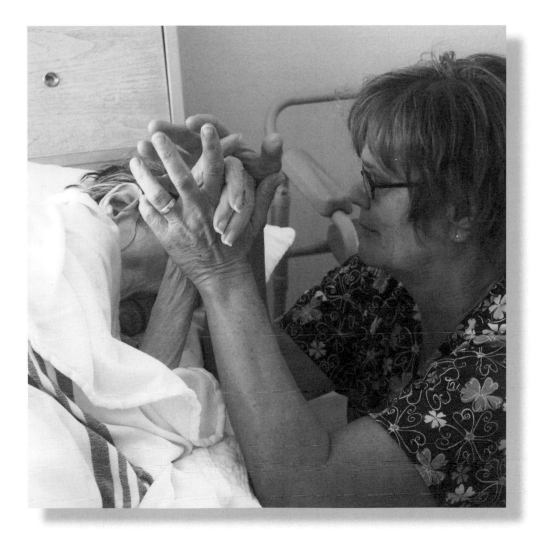

Richard hung his head, and I heard him start sniffling. His teary voice cracked. "Sorry I'm being so emotional. I just feel stuck inside. I have nobody." He had been living at a nursing home for about six weeks, and not by choice. His heart was failing, and he couldn't manage his apartment anymore.

I sparked a conversation about the only photo he had on his wall. Here he was seventeen years old and in middle of boot camp for the USAF. With a little coaxing, stories of Richard's life started joyfully pouring out of him. Richard's middle name was Harley. (His father owned a Harley Davidson shop.) In 1933 his father needed a change of scenery, so he attached a trailer with all their essential belongings to the back of his Harley and tucked a six-month-old Richard and his mother into a sidecar. They rode non-stop from Klamath Falls, Oregon to San Jose, California. Richard then reveled in his accomplishments as a lead machinist for a B-36 (the largest aircraft in the world at that time). He laughed as he told me stories of being a professional motorcycle racer, a proud and indispensible auto mechanic at the VA, and how he somehow wound up being a sewing machine repairman.

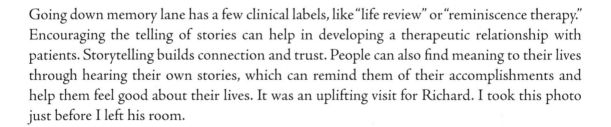

Going down memory lane has a few clinical labels, like "life review" or "reminiscence therapy." Encouraging the telling of stories can help in developing a therapeutic relationship with patients. Storytelling builds connection and trust. People can also find meaning to their lives through hearing their own stories, which can remind them of their accomplishments and help them feel good about their lives. It was an uplifting visit for Richard. I took this photo just before I left his room.

With a terminal diagnosis, a disruption in priorities, beliefs, and values often follows. After the initial shock, the terminally ill (and their families) often contemplate the purpose and meaning of their lives. Some rage about their suffering. The dying and their families often express anger at God for letting good people suffer.

In hospice we have a nursing diagnosis for this: spiritual distress.

What do I say to a thirty-something mother dying of ovarian cancer who screams at me in exhaustion about why this is happening to her?

What do I say to the somber twenty-something mother of a ten-month-old baby boy who can't love away his prognosis?

What words could soothe the distraught daughter of a dying father who is out of reach three thousand miles away?

I don't try to fix. I don't create a silver lining to any dark cloud of grief.

There is nothing to say, really. All I can do is provide a safe environment for however grief shows up, listen compassionately, and bear witness to the struggle. Sometimes sitting in silence is most comforting. I ask questions to offer the person more opportunity to reflect and express what they are feeling. I assure them that what they are feeling is normal.

Most folks who are angry or frustrated need to be seen and heard. We all want to say the right combination of words to make the people we care about feel better. Sometimes less is best.

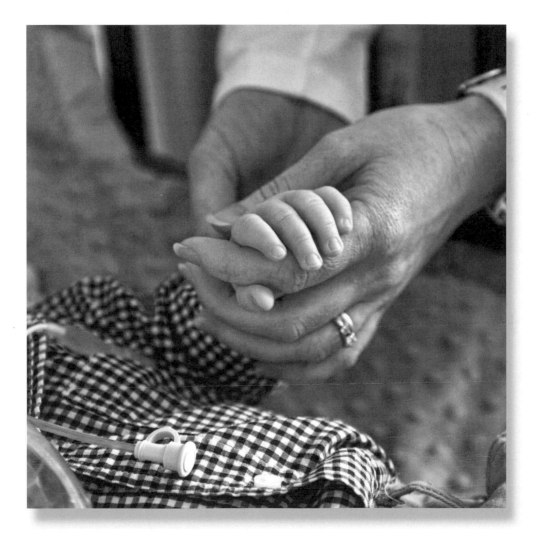

Edna wanted to go to Las Vegas and spend her money on the slots and then take in "one of those shows with naked ladies wearing feathered headdresses because the place will be crawling with available men." So we planned a fabulous trip to Las Vegas, where money was no object. Edna just turned ninety-five and had been happily living in a dementia unit for about five years.

The next time I came in to check on her she completely forgot our plan and didn't recognize me. Each week, much to her delight, she was "charmed" to meet me, and each week we planned the same trip to Las Vegas. She was (consistently) thrilled when I told her we would stay in the penthouse suite at the MGM Grand. Her only concern was if they would let her on the plane in a wheelchair. I told her we would take a private wheelchair-accessible jet. She predictably clapped her hands over her head as she insisted on getting her hair done first.

Edna had a lifetime of significant hardships that her dementia erased. According to her family, she was a defensive, suspicious woman, perhaps out of survival. When I was caring for her, she was happy, present, and joyous. The real Edna? She was without bad memories or resentments to dwell on and her only baggage was for her trip to Las Vegas.

Lucille's heart was nearly one hundred years old and failing. She could no longer venture out into the garden without great effort. Her daughter, Cynthia, brought the outside world into her mother's little apartment, and plants and flowers filled her room. She died on rose petals.

"My mom is the brightest star in my universe." ~Jean

There comes a time when the dying seem to have one foot firmly planted where they are headed next and the other uprooting from this world. They are commonly in a dream state, briefly in and out of awareness of their surroundings. I'm convinced that the dying review their lives carefully at this intriguing juncture.

Fond memories and passions are relived. A prize-winning quilter slowly stitched invisible fabric in the air in front of her chest. A retired ob-gyn carefully put on his gloves and positioned his hands to deliver a baby. A man who loved to fish cast his line carefully over and over. An opera singer led her orchestra with graceful hand motions holding her invisible baton with the tips of her delicate fingers.

Essential time is also spent in memories to resolve old issues (if any), to come to terms with life choices, or to take care of unfinished business. Here the dying can get restless, and some don't want to be touched. Offers for loving touch may be rejected, sometimes with aggression. Perhaps the dying simply don't want to be interrupted while they are doing the important work of closure.

I have sat quietly at the foot of deathbeds to witness the dying voice giving and receiving love and forgiveness. Here tears can finally shed, and an incredible peace can ensue. Most often it is in the stillness of resolve when the dying leave this world.

Sally had a busy ranch to run while losing the battle to an obstructive lung disease that eventually took her life (but not until she took care of all of her "business"). She had a fierce determination that no one could dampen. Short of breath, she said with a giggle, "I can't die until all my sheep have had their babies."

I enjoyed our visits. We sat in her kitchen while her beagles, Sophie and Willie Wonka, howled at the golden eagles that soared just outside her kitchen window. Anna, the yellow lab, chimed in too.

Sally was also a caregiver at a nursing facility I visited often. She cared for other people up until the last few months of her life.

This determined gal juggled it all with a feisty grace. She is missed terribly by many, never to be forgotten. Oh, and she was present for the birth of all of her sheep babies. She died shortly thereafter.

Ellie could remember the dress she wore on her fifth wedding anniversary back in 1949, but she could never recall who I was. Nearing the end stage of Alzheimer's, Ellie she was losing weight, getting weaker, and recently had to move from her family home into a locked dementia unit with twenty-four-hour caregivers.

Twice a week I introduced myself as a nurse and took Ellie's hand. Twice a week she expressed delight in meeting me. She silently held my gaze, then teared up and told me how beautiful I was and that she loved me. There was always a baby doll on her lap, and she always offered it to me to hold. I embraced the baby as if it were her own. It pleased Ellie.

Many of these special people say what they feel without social filters or political correctness. They appear to become egoless. Some spend their days in unresolved issues or struggles that aren't easy to identify from the outside looking in. Many with Alzheimer's, including Ellie, live in their true loving essence, sharing what they know to be true. In Ellie's case, she saw beauty in the world around her.

Ray was her knight in shining armor.

I followed the sounds of Carl's gentle sobs. His tears led me to the back bedroom, where his wife of sixty-two years made it home from the hospital just in time to die. Minutes after I arrived (and took this photo), she took her last breath. Carl held her right hand up to his cheek. His floodgates opened, and his river of tears ran down her arm. I sat quietly. Carl openly wept.

Our loving instinct is to hug, touch, or say something calming to someone who is crying uncontrollably. Sometimes it's best to do nothing but be completely present, allowing the grieving to cry and fully express their pain. Simply placing a silent hand on the grieving person's shoulder can actually interrupt and stop the release of their pain. This well intended interruption can shift focus. I've witnessed people stop crying, then apologize for their tears when given an unsolicited hug or even a tissue. It's a fine line, but an important one to consider. The right moment always comes to reach out with touch or words.

Fall in Love for the Day

If only for an hour
or several strung together
like clothes strung on a line,
hang your risk out to dry
along with all of your brilliant
reasons for pause.

The wind craves your caution.

Allow yourself to fall in love
hour to hour, end to end.

There is delight to be found
walking the tight rope
soaring high above the garden,

the glorious view
is God's blessing;
a promise that you are not lost.

From here you can only do
the right thing.

If you'd like,
you can have the safety net
of yesterday's loneliness
back under you feet
by tomorrow.

~From *Fear Means Go*
Poems and photography
by Mary Landberg

Linda died two times before being admitted to hospice, once from a heart attack and another time from a car accident. Clearly she needed to stick around a bit longer, as the CPR worked in both cases. In a fake southern accent she said, "Shucky darns, three times should be the charm." Her obstructive lung disease was nearing end stage. She was tired and ready to go, again.

Of course I asked her what it was like to die on those occasions. Linda looked like she was going to burst when she said ecstatically, "It was pure love, a peace beyond equal! Joy, oh the joy I felt! There was a light so bright it seemed like it could burn me, but it didn't. I'm looking forward to getting back there to stay."

She died for the last time several months after we met. I hope she made it to that loving, peaceful, joyous destination.

Maybelle was thrilled when she saw me photographing a family in the nursing home where she lived. She said with charming confidence that she wanted "a personal photo session." She took a moment to admire her long delicate ninety-one-year-old fingers and, without looking up, she said that she had never been a hand model and she wanted to take full advantage of the opportunity. I happily obliged. She was scheduled to be admitted to hospice that afternoon, as she had virtually stopped eating and drinking a few days prior.

Maybelle was happily living in memories of the glamorous lifestyle she led back in New York. She was a professional fragrance demonstrator at Macy's in the 1950s. Her hands danced in the air as she boasted about how exhausting it was. She then giggled. "Spritzing celebrities made it all worth it."

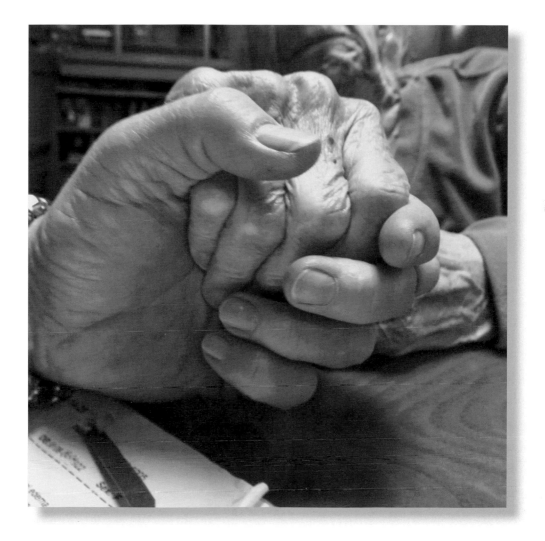

Sweet Anna lived in a locked dementia unit. Her caregivers called her Sweet Anna because if she were close enough to reach someone's hand, she would pull it up to her face and plant a slobbery kiss on it. She had a stroke, which left her weak on her right side. She had to be propped up with pillows while in her wheelchair.

Sweet Anna fell out of her wheelchair and broke her hip as she reached for her pillow that had fallen on the floor. After surgery she developed an infection that spread throughout her body. She was in horrible pain and was not expected to live through the week. Her son didn't want us to use anything stronger than Tylenol. He was adamant.

I stared at my pen for a moment, thinking about the implications of the ink I was ready to lay down on a hospice order at the skilled nursing facility. My pen has significant power; I have to be very careful with it. It is rarely my intention to sedate anybody. I typically start pain medicine at a low dose, then titrate the dose up until pain relief has been reached. Sometimes the amount of pain medicine it takes to dull the pain can cause drowsiness. Occasionally the amount of medicine needed can put someone into a deep sleep.

This is difficult for some families to accept. They would rather have their loved one live their final days in pain and awake versus pain free and possibly sedated. I am a strong advocate for my patients who can't speak for themselves and I do everything in my power to educate families about comfort care. In this case, I firmly suggested to the son that I break his hip and offer him only Tylenol.

Anna died completely peaceful with dignity and grace. Pain free.

I could barely fit through the door of the vintage silver Airstream camper permanently parked behind a hedge of poplar trees by the river. Cheryl's queen-sized bed took up half the space inside. A big bed is what Cheryl wanted. Her dear friend Earl saw to it that she got everything she needed. She was dying from pancreatic cancer.

Earl stood nearly seven feet tall. His scruffy salt and pepper beard was as long as his spindly pony tail, which landed in the middle of his muscular back. The weathered red bandana tied tight around his head was saturated with weeks, maybe months, of sweat. Obscenities were tattooed on both forearms and knuckles. He wore a fringed, black leather jacket and chaps over his dirty, worn-out jeans. I could hear his Harley crackle outside as it cooled off.

Earl met me at Cheryl's place to talk about starting hospice care. I'd never seen fingernails as dirty as Earl's when he reached out to shake my hand for the first time. Earl could intimidate the toughest of us. In times like these, something soft can happen to the rough edges of the seemingly hardened. The ego can shatter when it comes to urgent matters of the heart. Vulnerability finally becomes obvious when the harshest of souls realize their tough exteriors can't change the outcome of terminal disease. Layers of a lifetime of hardship can fall away; love is all that matters. We are all the same in this way.

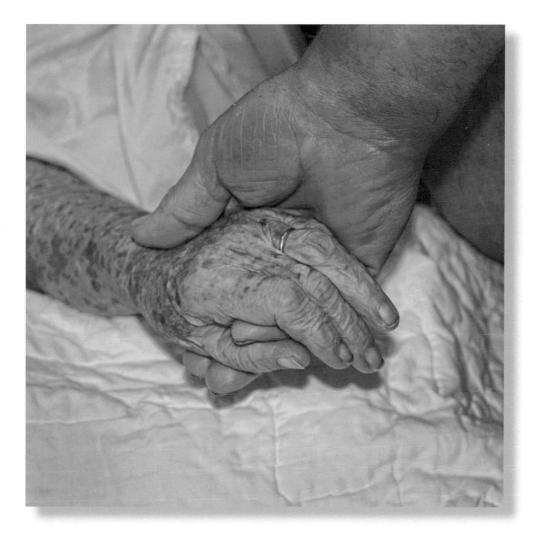

Several decades ago she took a risk and wrote him a long love letter explaining her feelings that had been growing since she sat in his audience at a brilliant lecture he gave at Duke University. Such risks are clearly worth taking. She got the attention of his heart with her humbling honesty. They were inseparable for the best forty years of their lives.

Ralph asked Carol to marry him on their first date, nearly sixty years ago. Love at first sight indeed exists. Their regular public displays of affection gave well received permission for others to do the same.

Openly and frequently express your love for the people you care about. Carol said, "Never assume that your loved ones know how you feel."

We should all have one person who knows how to bless us despite the evidence. Grandmas are like that.

Sandy spent the last three nights in the ancient high-back armchair next to her mother's bed. Sandy's vigil was taking a significant toll on her on many levels. I met her on the morning of the fourth day. It looked like Sandy was holding her breath in between inhalations. Her furrowed brow, rigid posture, and the bloodshot sorrow in her eyes told her story.

It was clear to me that this was her mother's last day of life. When I told Sandy this, tears poured down her face as she chewed off the last bits of her fingernails on her right hand. She hopelessly sobbed. "My mother is my best friend. What will I do without her? She is the person who helps me through difficult times in my life. I have nobody to turn to."

In that moment it would have been pointless to offer suggestions on how to find meaning in her life after her mother died.

My response was, "Tell me about your mother." As her sweet stories unfolded I saw Sandy's shoulders relax, her breathing changed, and the furrow of her brow unraveled a little. Then it was my mission to make Sandy chuckle. By the end of my visit we both laughed at how Sandy and her mother would tape paper plates to the bottoms of their feet and play "ice skater" in their kitchen.

Storytelling is powerful medicine for grief.

These brothers hadn't been in each other's company in well over a decade. They came together on this day of their father's passing. They held hands and lovingly supported each other despite the years of separation.

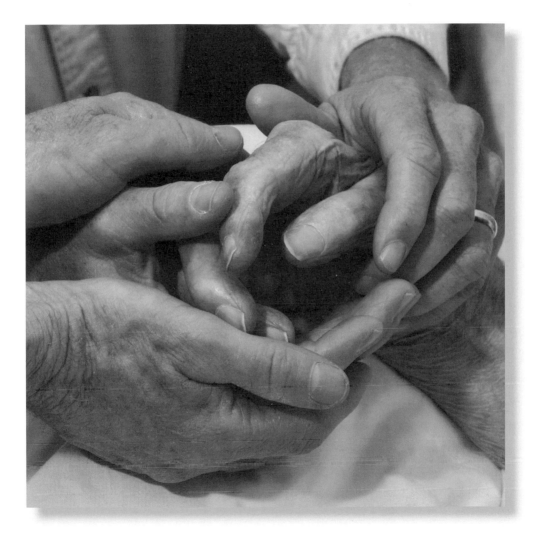

Flo was a remarkable woman. She was wheelchair-bound with cerebral palsy since early childhood. She spent the last thirty-three years of her life living in a skilled nursing facility and completely dependent on others for all of her physical needs. She said she wouldn't trade her living situation or her body for anything different.

She easily won the hearts of many with her consistent selfless acts of love for others. For instance, she arranged aluminum can drives within her nursing home and gave the profits "to the needy."

Flo attracted a caliber of people in her life that I believe most long for. Bearing witness to the consistent unconditional love and genuine dedication from her friends was nearly overwhelming. Flo will forever be known to her community as the "Oracle of Love."

At eighteen, Laura saw a need for a schoolhouse in Benton, Kansas, so she built one. This lovely lady held thousands of five-year-old hearts, hands, and minds during her fifty-year career as a kindergarten teacher. She proudly spoke of her mission of teaching young children self-sufficiency, self-respect, and doing for others.

Most of us have had one teacher that made a significant difference in our lives. Most great teachers don't get that feedback. Teachers are our unsung heroes. Who was that teacher for you?

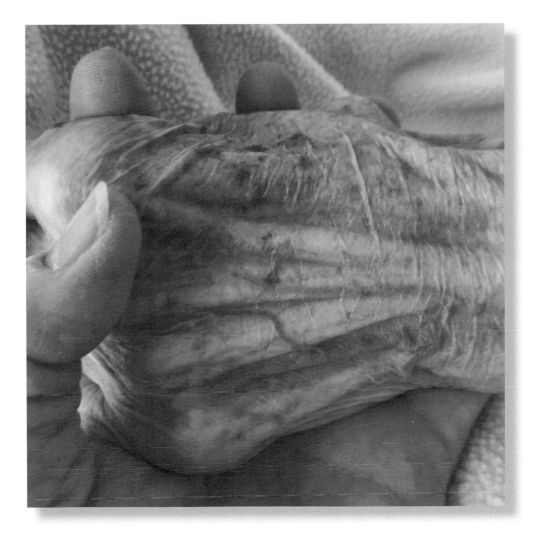

Hilda stabbed her husband of forty-five years in the back with a butcher knife as he was bending over to pick something up in the garage. Richard's left lung was pierced, and he quickly collapsed. He crawled into the house and headed for their bedroom to call an ambulance. She followed him in a rage and ready to strike again. While she held the knife high above her head, Richard reached for the gun in his nightstand and shot a bullet into the floor in hopes of stopping her from stabbing him again. Hilda lunged forward. Richard shot her. The bullet ripped through her left wrist and into her hip. She fell to the floor, then got back up, knife still in hand. Her daughter burst in the door and convinced Hilda to drop the knife. The police and ambulance arrived shortly thereafter.

Hilda had been diagnosed with a rapid onset form of Lewy Body dementia six months prior to this event. She refused treatment, and Richard kept her secret for too long. He loved her so much and didn't want to release her to a supervised dementia facility, where she really needed to be.

That horrific incident was in October of last year. Hilda is now in a dementia facility bound to a wheelchair and on hospice. Richard comes in every day to hold her hand and stroke her hair. He stays for hours. She rarely recognizes him. His love for her is stronger than the behavior of her disease.

Many decades ago Stan went to the Long Beach Veterans Administration every Sunday to volunteer his time for his fellow World War II veterans. They were all bed-bound with recent wounds of war. Stan would release the brakes on their beds and roll them one by one out of their rooms and down the hall to the movie theater for a change of scenery and pace. Stan was honored and delighted to be a "bed roller."

As a culture we have been trained to hold back our tears. A surprising number of people hide their vulnerability this way, and if a tear slips out, they will immediately apologize for crying. Tears have certain wisdom.

Tears that spill in response to emotional pain are very different in composition from tears that fall in response to joy or peeling an onion. Tears of sadness contain the release of stress hormones and natural painkillers. This may be why having "a good cry" feels good.

I encourage all not to fight the urge to cry. It's the body's innate wisdom offering a healthy way to express emotion. Shedding tears openly also gives others permission to do the same. It's also okay for hospice nurses to shed a tear or two, as I did while photographing this beautiful family.

As a young adult, Janice watched her grandfather endure dementia from its frustrating onset to the grizzly last moments of his life. Recently, in her late seventies, Janice recognized the same early symptoms surfacing in herself. She was unwilling to go to her doctor, because she feared the probable prognosis. She did her best to hide her symptoms. She coped with her secret through behaviors. A point came when her husband couldn't take care of her anymore, or keep her secret for her. She was placed in a locked care facility.

She became an escape artist. On several occasions she confidently walked out the front door alongside an unsuspecting visitor. She paid close attention to the combinations of buttons the visitors pushed to unlock the doors. She then found the perfect timing to dash outside—when the staff was busy with other residents. She picked locks, ripped through screens, and broke windows for a brief chance to wander the neighborhood. On one occasion a neighbor lady invited her in for coffee, then soon realized she was very confused, so she called the police. Janice was always completely willing to come back to the facility and she never put up a fight.

Finding a way out was the only sense of accomplishment she had at that point in her life.

Elizabeth is a music-thanatologist. She delivers an integral form of end-of-life care that complements our medicine in beautiful harmony. She plays her soul-stirring harp and passionately sings for the dying and their loved ones.

Her live music is individually tailored and prescriptive, meaning that it changes from moment to moment based on the needs of the patient. Elizabeth's enchanting arrangements help ease restlessness, labored breathing, and pain. I've witnessed her music instantly create a soothing environment of calm for families (and hospice nurses) too.

I enjoy reading her poetic narratives that follow her visits with our hospice patients. Here is an excerpt: "Music begins with a gentle waltz in a major key. The patient closes his eyes and the music flows into a minor key, supporting the shift to more interiority. A flowing Celtic tune played rubato offers support for relaxation, moving into improvisation. The patient's posture softens. Another minor key Celtic tune flows into an unmetered chant. I pause and reach one hand out, which he grabs. We swing arms gently back and forth and I hum an improvised waltz as our arms dance. The patient chuckles."

At sixteen, Walter went out of his way daily to walk by Venida's high school classroom to catch a glimpse of her smiling face. He didn't know it, but Venida would purposefully sit by the window so he could see her. One day Venida wasn't at the window. Walter quickly learned that her family had to leave town permanently due to a family emergency. It took weeks for Walter to find her, and they finally met face to face.

I asked Walter if it was love at first sight back at the high school window. He tearfully replied, "Oh yes. I haven't recovered yet, and we've been together sixty-eight years."

Hollywood portrays death in overly dramatic ways to sell movie tickets. Nearly all people on hospice (regardless of cause of death) take their last breath the same way, peacefully in their sleep.

There are some circumstances where people don't go peacefully. Those with a strong history of substance abuse, anger, or a stressful lifestyle tend to have a harder time letting go. High-strung types can need a lot of control in the dying process, and easygoing types tend to roll with the punches. It's almost like people die the way they live.

He was an American cultural and literary historian, author of over twenty books, university professor to decades of eager students, and, most important, madly in love with Harriette.

"We cried when we first saw the portrait of our hands. We held hands and hugged a lot until Ray died a month later. The photograph sits in my living room where I can see it every day. I show it to everyone. It warms my heart to do so. It is the one thing that I cherish most; it keeps Ray here."

~Sheila

This is one of my first hand portraits. When I received this note,
I knew I had to keep doing this!

Catherine was on stage singing and dancing two weeks prior to this photograph. One hundred and fifty close friends and family were partying along with her as she celebrated her one hundredth year. She suffered a massive stroke shortly afterward. Her four daughters continued the celebration of her life at her bedside. Her amazing long life was well worth rejoicing.

Paul was known as a "maverick warrior of the heart." I asked Paul's beloved wife, Anya, what this means. She proudly said, "Paul always referred to himself as a maverick, one who shoots from the hip and lives outside the box. He had an uncanny sense with people, especially men. He led from the heart. The men he mentored always felt safe with him. He had a way of cracking open even the toughest of veneers. So many men said to me, 'Paul changed my life and gave me back a piece of myself I didn't even know I had lost.' The last six months of his life he often said, 'I've become the man I've always wanted to be.' I watched him traverse the realms until he was comfortable enough to let go of his earthly body. I was honored to be his partner."

It was the second time in two weeks Gary found himself behind her in line at the Nordstrom Cafe in the Washington Mall in Portland, Oregon. He took that as a sign he was meant to know this beautiful woman. She said yes to coffee that rainy fall day in November of 1979. They said yes to marriage four months later.

Gary said tearfully, "Martie was diagnosed with early onset Alzheimer's in 2002 at the age of fifty-eight. She has been living in this locked dementia facility for the last ten years. It is difficult to say if she recognizes me. She stopped saying my name two years ago. I still come every day and feed her lunch. She knows that someone who loves her is here. This is what I can do for my sweetheart."

This daughter of this dying mother told me I offer "quite a ministry." I thought a personal ministry was about sharing religious teachings. Perhaps not always.

My ministry is to photograph loving people holding the hands of their dying beloveds, to help keep their memory alive after they have passed. It feels good to say that my ministry is to share my gifts and experiences to reach others in a positive, loving way. Maybe I was given this passion for photography for this reason.

I think we all have a ministry to offer.

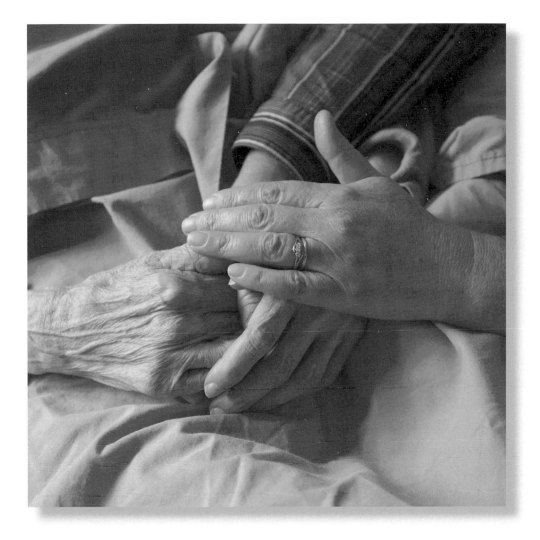

When hospice walks in the door for the first time, our presence is the death sentence verified. It becomes real. Someone in the house is going to die. At first the dying person is the primary focus. We evaluate head to toe and develop a comprehensive, holistic plan of care that takes into account physical, spiritual, emotional, and social needs.

Once the patient's immediate needs are accommodated, the focus of care broadens to include the family. We focus on the grieving family as much as the dying patient. The anticipation of death triggers the grieving process, which can bring out the best and worst in people. There is an urgency to resolve old issues, take care of unfinished business, and give or receive forgiveness.

I am honored to help families get through such urgent matters of the mind so that they can focus on what matters most. Love—it's all that is left in the end.

Paul was a big man in many ways. He never complained about his cancer pain and asked for little. He was bed-bound in a cramped little room he rented in a shed behind a fancy restaurant. Despite Paul's obvious poverty, he always found something to offer the hospice staff: tap water in a recycled paper cup, an aging banana, or an article he enjoyed in an old *New Yorker*. Paul was a true giver.

He consistently refused gourmet meals offered to him by the restaurant owner. But if friends dropped by with Jack in the Box, he would gladly accept. He didn't want handouts; he honored reciprocation.

Karyl was in her early fifties and diagnosed with end stage ovarian cancer. Her brother Mike was (to say the least) a health enthusiast. He insisted that three times a day, for a year, she drink a medicinal tea that comes from a special village in India. He was certain it would reverse her advanced cancer. Karyl refused to drink more than one sip of the tea as she found it to taste like cat pee. Mike wouldn't take no for an answer. Their relationship became strained.

Family and friends can experience intense frustration when the dying don't take their well intended advice. We think we know what's best for the people we love (and sometimes for strangers too). Maybe we've "been there, done that" and know probable outcomes from experience.

Here is my unsolicited advice to take or leave. Ask the dying (or anyone in struggle), "What is the most loving thing I can do for you right now?" Honor the answer, even if it's, "I need to be alone."

When Hal auditioned for the choir as a baritone, he didn't think that fateful day in 1962 would change his life forever.

He beamed as he said, "When our eyes met for the first time, I had to know everything about her. I discovered Martha for fifty beautiful years." Hal's tears flowed freely and joyfully when he spoke of his grand love for Martha.

Martha was not only a talented soprano, but a gifted poet who won national awards on a regular basis. Hal kept Martha's poetry alive by memorizing her favorite pieces. He recited them to her daily with a passionate fervor that moved me to tears. She appeared not to recognize Hal or her own beautiful poetry, but there was a familiar twinkle in her steel blue eyes that kept him coming back to the dementia unit twice a day until the day she died.

With regularity I'm asked the question, "When is my mother going to die?" My answer can trigger a phone tree that immediately puts people on airplanes all over the country. My answer initiates a huge shift in priorities, and people give a moment's notice to their employers and families. Loved ones drop everything and come.

I'd better be right. Right? Most folks follow the textbook in a predictable sequence in their decline, but some don't. If I'm wrong about timing, it's never a bad idea to come visit your loved ones. Right?

I have predicted that someone would die within hours to a day or two, and they live over a week, then die seconds after a loved one finally arrives to say goodbye. Would they have died at the same moment regardless of their last visitor? I have seen people die moments after I have assured their family they might have weeks of life left. Can a sense of completion of life allow release?

I have observed people who have lived tragic lives struggle emotionally until the absolute end, well after their body should have died. Can unfinished business keep us alive? Some families hold twenty-four-hour bedside vigils because they don't want their beloved to die alone. Sometimes, after days of vigil, the family leaves the room to run an errand or get coffee, and that is when the dying take their last breath. Alone.

Do we have an emotional body that has a will of its own? Do we have some control over when we take our last breath?

When I ask dying people what they would miss most about their life, I hear things like "Belly laughs at the kitchen table. We laughed so hard we cried when Uncle Tom strolled into the kitchen with half his beard shaved off." The kitchen seems to be the place so many happy memories are made. "The best birthday cake Mom ever made me was the one that sunk in the middle and we filled in the hole with plastic flowers." I hear about many grand family gatherings to celebrate life. "We all sang Motown tunes during dinner around Aunt Mary's kitchen table while she danced like nobody was watching. Soon we were all jumping around the kitchen doing the twist."

People share how they joyfully grew and maintained connection while playing cards and board games at Grandma's, gave and received the best advice over tea, and held "deep heart-to-heart conversations over sister's secret recipe for chocolate chip pecan cookies."

These are clearly the most important memories worth making.

When I ask people who are not on their deathbed about their priorities in life, they usually speak of spending quality time with family, getting in better physical condition, traveling, writing that book, getting a better job, or saving money. When I ask them what they did after work the night before, I usually hear, "I watched TV for a couple of hours." Their priority was clearly watching TV.

What fond memories are you making with your beloveds?

Once a week Bernice whispered to me in a giggle, "Did you know that I am engaged to be married in three weeks?" Well into her nineties, she consistently fell in love with the male caregivers at the dementia unit where she lived, the same three twenty-something, good-humored guys. Bernice would bat her eyes, look all shy, and offer her big, bright, toothless smile whenever they passed by.

She had married young, spent decades with an abusive husband, and also said weekly, "I am still looking for that special someone to treat me right."

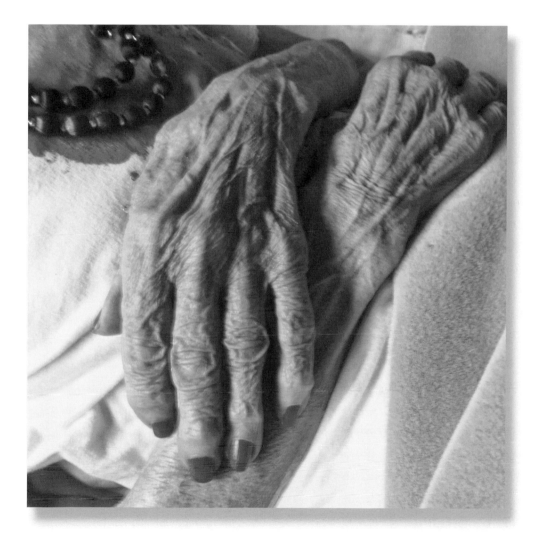

"I am not wealthy. I am rich in family and experiences." ~Roscoe

Bob's oncologist gave him up to fourteen days to live; his biweekly blood transfusions were no longer effective at keeping him from severe, debilitating fatigue.

Bob had the sense of humor of a healthy man and an upbeat acceptance of his prognosis as if he had a whole life ahead of him. He chuckled, "Well, I never have to do laundry again! When I am done wearing something, I'll just toss it in the trash."

Laughter is potent medicine for stress, pain, and conflict. A good laugh can bring the mind back to focus, can lighten mood, and deepen connections between people. Studies have shown than laughter has beneficial effects on the body, including increased oxygen use, which leads to better circulation, reduced pain, increased pain tolerance, and relaxation.

It is always one of my goals to make my hospice patients and families laugh. Bob made reaching this goal easy. Laughter enhances the quality of life. Of course there are times when laughter would be inappropriate, but when opportunities present themselves, don't use it sparingly.

The Threshold Singers are a group of lovely, dedicated women who sing a capella at the bedside of people struggling—some with living, some with dying. They offer their song as a gift to those they beautifully serenade.

Most are moved to stillness when they hear the group's big hearts overflow through their sweet, compassionate voices. I stop and take them in no matter how busy I am. These gals are truly medicine for the heart and soul.

Shirley owned Carousel Hair Fashion in Walnut Creek, California, during the big hair days of the 1960s. Shirley couldn't take walk-ins, as her chair was booked six months in advance. Her voluminous updos and beehives took the meaning of bouffant to new heights. Shirley's handiwork made a significant difference in the lives she touched with her talent, teasing comb, and hairspray. Shirley was an artist, and a physicist of sorts.

Could the single occurrence of a great hairdo change the emotional course of Walnut Creek? Think about it. A grumpy gal walks into her salon with unruly hair and consequent low self-esteem. She walks out feeling beautiful and confident. Her improved mood is shared with her immediate world, and a happy ripple effect begins. We are kinder people when we are happy.

Go get your hair done.

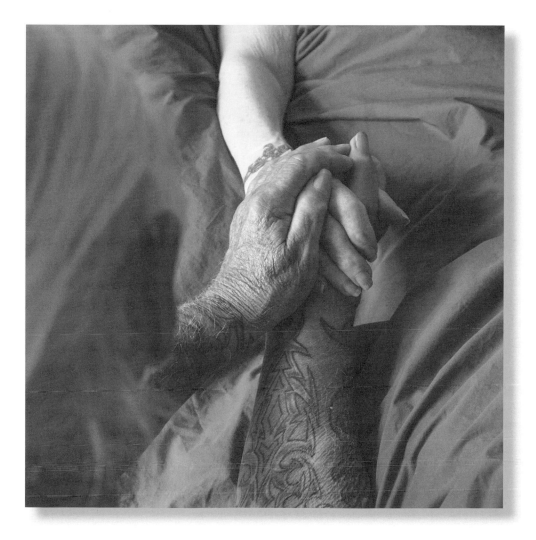

For many people, a referral to hospice is the first introduction to end of life. What happens next can bring out the best qualities in people, call forth the worst, and most have some level of worry, fear of the unknown, and every emotion in between.

When I walk in the door for the first time, I am often met with emotionally distraught people, spinning in different directions, colliding with one another (literally and figuratively). Family members commonly have a deer-in-the-headlights look on their faces, their shoulders hiked up near their ears, and are unable to fully exhale.

When we are in worry, fear, or physical or emotional pain, it can consume us, and we find ourselves not being able to think or deal with anything else.

This is when the most gratifying part of my job as a hospice nurse comes in.

I have the family gather, often around the bed of the loved one who is dying. I talk about what is happening, why it's happening, what to expect in the next moments, hours, or days, and what the last breath looks like. Most hang onto every word with open mouths. I offer opportunities to ask questions, and beautiful discussions follow. I have had these discussions hundreds of times.

When the dying process is no longer a scary mystery, people can get to what matters most. To me, that is connection and love.

Bernadette was the wheelchair race champion of the nursing home, hands down.

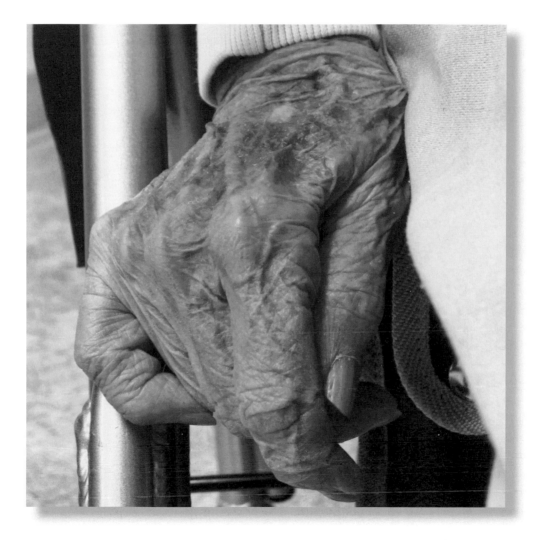

Typically a family member serves as the primary caregiver for a dying loved one. Living rooms turn into hospital rooms. These often-untrained caregivers have to make key medical decisions, sometimes hourly. The process of caregiving can be extremely stressful and chaotic. Caregivers get so busy caring for others that they may neglect their own physical and emotional health. Giving can also be a way of coping.

Caregiver burnout is real, for caregivers at home with a loved one and for professionals caring for many elderly residents at a time. Here are some questions you can ask yourself or someone you know to determine if they are headed towards caregiver burnout. Do you feel like you are always riding an emotional roller coaster? Are you often irritable, anxious, and gloomy? Do you get sick often? Stress not only breeds depression and anxiety, it can weaken your immune system so you catch every bug that crosses your path and you stay sick longer. If you have a day off, do you still think about and process occurrences and problems of caregiving? Is your appetite poor? Do you have trouble thinking straight? Are you exhausted even after a good night's sleep?

Here is what I know for sure: You can't take good care of anyone if you don't take good care of yourself. Period. Just imagine the additional stress and frustration you would feel if you were confined to bed sick and you had to quickly arrange for someone else take care of your loved one. In many cases this would be a stranger from an agency that you wouldn't have the time to interview for a good fit.

What would you tell a caregiver headed toward burnout?

Earl's friends said he could fix anything with a Swiss army knife, a couple large paperclips, and some WD-40, which he always had tucked in one of his large pockets of his overalls. He was MacGyver personified. He loved to tinker with old cars. He had a little shop on his property where he spent all of his waking hours. He would also take long naps there, surrounded by his beloved car parts.

On my third visit he really opened up to me. He confessed how he really felt. This is when I learned that he expressed himself best by swearing. He said, "I could hardly get my sorry little *%&$ out of my &%^$ bed this morning. What the &*#@ is wrong with me?" Earl was clearly frustrated about how his body wouldn't let him do what he used to do. He didn't understand and was spitting fire mad. Earl was ninety-six.

I tailored what I had to say to a level that he could understand and in a way that wasn't overwhelming. For Earl, I chose to talk about his body using car part metaphors.

I told him, "Parts are parts, they wear out. The parts in your car wear out after so many miles, and the parts in your body wear out after so many years." I spoke of his own exhaust system, gas tank, fuel pump, carburetor, electrical system, and lubrication. He got it.

Is there a message you are trying to get across that needs to be delivered in a different way?

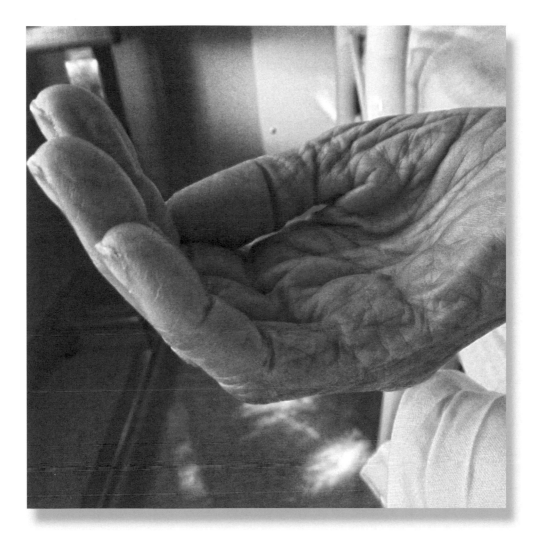

Hospice patients will share their deepest secrets and most distressing stories with me, often within the first hour of our first meeting. I don't know why hospice nurses are a safe place to land hard truths and confidences that have been kept private for decades. Hospice nurses are intimate strangers.

I wasn't sure how to respond to Jack's confessions of Mafia involvement in New York City during the 1950s. He shared how tough he had to be to survive and protect his family. Providing for his wife and three children was his duty and the reason he took significant risks. He bowed his head when he said he had to hurt people to prevent harm to himself and his family.

The day came when Jack couldn't get out of bed anymore. His cancer had taken what was left of his independence. In a moment of total acceptance of his impending death, he turned his head away from me in shame as he tearfully confessed that he felt like a failure, as he couldn't protect and provide for his family anymore. He felt he had no purpose.

I offered the idea that perhaps he had protected and provided his family into resilient independence and now his job was done. He agreed with a smirk of acknowledgment of this truth.

I was deeply moved to learn that before he died, he dictated letters to his family and included photographs that I had taken as a farewell gesture and confirmation of his life successfully complete.

"When my mom was near the end she would call me 'Mama.' At first I was alarmed and a bit heartbroken . . . I prayed to know what to do. The next time it happened, I held her hand and said, 'I'm here, Pet.' ('Pet' was a term of endearment my grandmother used.) Calmness immediately came over her. From then on, I was no longer scared, and my mom was more peaceful." ~Jane

When we were young children, most of us innately called out for our mothers if we needed help, love, comfort, or if we were bursting at our seams with pride and needed to share our joy. A fair percentage of the dying also call out for their mothers while in that deep dream state prior to passing. When this happens, often with beautiful effect, I whisper into their ear, "Mommy is here. You are safe. I love you."

It appears that the unconditional comfort we found in our mothers as children never fades entirely, even if it gets buried under daily distractions or ego. Some of us have to mother ourselves through difficult times. Perhaps as healthy adults we have a longing for the safety of this forgotten comfort, but we just can't identify it as such.

This lovely married couple spent their last few years living together in a locked dementia unit, unable to care for themselves anymore and unable to recognize each other, or so it was thought.

Some days they were wheeled by each other, and they did not give each other even a glance of recognition, and other days he openly confessed his love for her out loud for everyone to witness. Sometimes without words spoken, they would gaze into each other's eyes with sincere, whole-hearted devotion.

He died first. She followed suit within a year. It is not uncommon for one spouse to follow the other into hospice, and for both to die within a short span of time.

Can we die of a broken heart?

Family members and friends from all over the country drop everything and come. The urgency of arrival is in the hope of doing this … one more time.

Morris was a celebrated and renowned FBI agent. He was proud to say that he "thrived in dangerous situations." He felt "important." He loved to travel the country and solve complicated mysteries, and he was very paid well for it. His huge home and accumulation of things were his proof of success. But, according to him, they lost their meaning. At eighty-two, he confined himself to his room and was dependent on oxygen. He could no longer walk without being short of breath, and his vision and hearing were "shit." He felt he no longer had a purpose. He told us he was simply "waiting to die."

In our culture, most value and identify themselves by what they do or by what they have. Once we stop producing and accumulating, we can lose our purpose, meaning, and value.

Many have told me they find meaning and purpose in raising a family, growing spiritually, reaching career goals, exploration, learning new skills, creativity, giving back, and in being useful. Who are we when our children grow up, when we retire, or when we get sick and we lose the use of our bodies, eyes, or ears?

When our bodies can no longer *do* for us, our task becomes how can we value *being* in our body and in the world. In our culture, we typically don't value people who are being.

What does it mean to be?

People don't sign up for hospice because they want to die. While they are on our service, we help them live their best possible life while they make the unavoidable journey toward death.

"You live everyday. You only die once."
~Unknown

"I don't want to be a burden on my family," she said in a hoarse whisper. The tumor in her throat was compromising her speech, breathing, and ability to swallow. She had been given about thirty days to live. Yet she hid her growing despair and worst pain when her family was present.

I asked her to tell me about the joy of taking care of her four children during those hard economic times of their youth. She sometimes worked two jobs to make ends meet. She sacrificed sleep and her personal health so that they would have healthy food to eat and a safe, loving place to live. She sparkled, "I wouldn't have traded those years for anything. I love my children so much. They were an incredible joy."

I offered her the idea of letting her children have the same opportunity to receive incredible joy by allowing them to take care of her. By refusing their care, by not wanting to be a burden, she could be returning a beautiful gift unopened. In receiving, we give joy.

My words made sense to her, and she spent the last days of her life demonstrating to her adult children how to receive. It was a most heartwarming joy to witness.

Very young children know themselves to be light and love. If we allow them, maybe they can teach us to see ourselves the same way.

Perhaps this is why sweet baby Elizabeth came into this family for such a short time.

Sal's cardiologist told him his medications were no longer working, and at ninety-seven, heart surgery was out of the question. His doctor also gently suggested that Sal's implanted defibrillator be turned off and he allow hospice to step in. Sal was thrilled.

He was done living, but his body wasn't. He could hang on for a few more months or more. The worst part was that he "couldn't do anything for anyone anymore." He spent his days "waiting to die."

Sal's eyes were so bad he couldn't read or watch TV anymore, and his hearing aids weren't effective even when turned up all the way. He became very short of breath with minimal exertion. He catnapped about fourteen hours each day. Nothing tasted good anymore; he ate out of boredom. Sal had a quick wit and mentally was as sharp as a tack.

I offered Sal the idea of living while he was still alive. He rolled his eyes and grumbled that he was, "Open to ideas." When he got home from the hospital, I arranged for his caregiver to take him on daily smell-walks. It was the perfect time of year for it. So his caregiver put him in his wheelchair, and they were off to neighboring gardens. He was so pleased. After his first smell-walk, he reported that he had been alive close to one hundred years and had never taken the time to fully take in the smell of lavender, rosemary, pine needles, or lilac.

Daily, Jacquelene went beyond the call of duty for her dying sister. She went enough extra miles to wear out the soles of one hundred pair of running shoes.

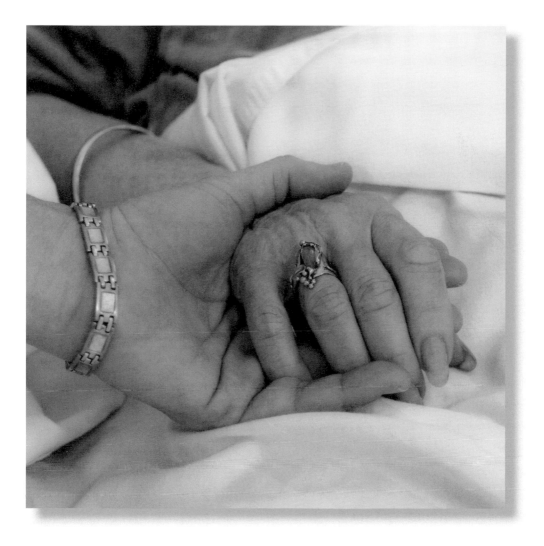

John had been saying goodbye to his father for almost a year and was exhausted on many levels. His father had been in and out of the hospital in critical condition several times in eleven months. With each hospital admission, doctors told John that his father was going to die in a few days. John had a feeling that this would be the last goodbye. He was right.

I wish I had a crystal ball to predict when people will die. Sometimes I can, if they follow the textbook. Many don't.

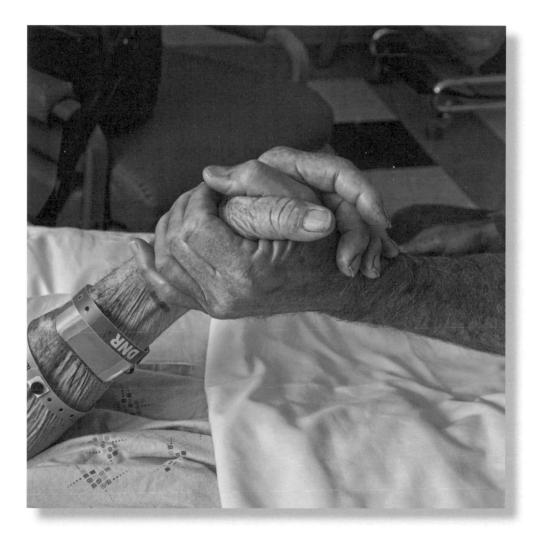

Hanging on to old grudges is a recurring theme for the bed-bound. Grudges distance us from the people we love and need the most. Sometimes these grudges are unconsciously held and manifest as an uncomfortable awkwardness between people.

I dug deeper into the resentment between a father and son. I learned from the father that the distance between them had grown over the last fifteen years because the son never made his final payment on a stereo system that the father had sold him out of desperation to pay bills. With clenched teeth, the father told me, "I really needed that money to pay my hospital bill, and the lazy bastard couldn't come up with a hundred bucks?" His son had no idea this was the reason his father had been giving him the cold shoulder over the years. He thought his father was "evolving into a grumpy old man." With this realization, both sprung into tears, both let go of their pain.

Have you been carrying around an unnecessary grudge that is preventing you from giving and receiving loving fully?

Bernard confessed to me that he didn't think his prayers were good enough. "I wasn't taught how to pray properly," he said. He expressed remorse because "At twelve years old I started liking downhill skiing better than going to church on Sundays." I asked him if he believed that only the poetic, articulate people get their prayers heard. He said, "How does God know what I need to communicate if I can't say it right?"

I presented the idea of not saying words during prayer. Bernard's eyes grew wide. He furrowed his brow and cocked his head to the side. I had him close his eyes and bring his attention to the feeling of what he wanted to pray about. No words, just the feeling. With a little guidance, he found the feeling. By the way he relaxed and nodded his head, I could see he was in the middle of it. I suggested he give that feeling to God, offer the feeling as a prayer, which was already being answered. It made sense to him that if God is able to interpret all 6,500 languages spoken on this planet, God can interpret honest feelings without words attached.

Bernard was relieved and said he hoped God understood that all he wanted was his wife to be safe after he died.

When I Am Silent

When I am silent
I am abled.

When I am silent
I am able to see
the barbed ache
oozing from the massive
crack in your chest.

When I am silent
I am able to taste
the salty fear politely
leaking from
the shame in your face.

When I am silent
I am able to hold
this delicate container
for your stubborn vulnerability
to trickle into.

When I am silent
I am able to feel
your defenses melt
as I stroke your forehead
when nobody is watching.

~From *Fear Means Go*
Poetry and photography
by Mary Landberg

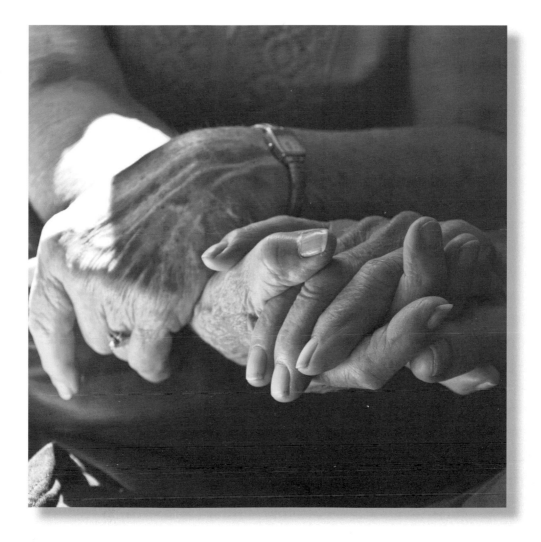

People implode; neglect will do that. It doesn't happen often, but we find elders left virtually forgotten in a back bedroom or garage of a broken-down home where household members could really care less. The lack of care and love can drive a person inward. Despite horrific circumstances, some of these elderly people find peace within. They withdraw completely from the outside world to cope. It's a tragic set of circumstances to walk into.

With a few swift phone calls, our hospice team can quickly get these deserving people into the loving hands of a nursing home or foster care. We have had several cases like these where elders have flourished with hospice involvement and recovered enough to not need our help anymore. Hospice workers advocate for life.

One of the most rewarding qualities of my job as a hospice worker is to help families move through blocks that can prevent them from expressing what they feel. When love is finally able to flow freely, all that doesn't matter has the invitation to melt away. Expressing love provides a magnificent opportunity to heal at these times of the unknown.

"There is nothing more to do and nowhere else to go." ~Mira Sophia

Our lives can seem to be a collection of losses, big and small. We graduate from school, leave home, change jobs, parents divorce, relationships break up, our children leave the house, we lose social circles, pets die, friends move away, we age, and most lose physical strength and endurance. Some people die suddenly, and for some, it takes years in anticipation.

Could we all be walking around carrying heavy suitcases of unresolved grief without realizing it?

Grief comes and goes in waves, tsunami style at first (depending on the loss). Grieving people can live their lives while having difficulty concentrating, while feeling sad, depressed, irritable, anxious, ambivalent, frustrated, and while lacking motivation and energy. These symptoms can resolve over time, but for some they never go away. These emotions can be well or partially hidden under the busyness of our lives.

So what do we do with these feelings? Acknowledge them, feel them, be with them, discuss them, and express them. Be patient with yourself. Resolution could take a day, a month, a year, or more.

Some people start living only when they get sick. For some it takes a cancer diagnosis to start appreciating and taking care of their body. Why do some people have to get sick or injured to finally lie down and rest?

Our culture tends to believe that pain is a natural part of the aging process. It's true that older adults are more likely to experience pain, but it's not true that pain is inevitable as we age. I spend my days with the over-eighty crowd, and not all of them are experiencing pain. A fair percentage of elderly have pain related to wear and tear on joints and the common aches and pains of immobility. Often, over-the-counter pain medications ease such pains. For those who aren't treated, their pain can take center stage. They don't want to get out of bed or participate in personal care.

Think about the last time you were in pain, maybe broke your toe, hurt your back, or had a bad headache. You probably couldn't think or deal with much else. Our pain can consume us. We may prefer to curl up in a ball in bed and insist on being left alone.

Just think of the elderly who have, say, untreated chronic inflammation in their joints. Of course they aren't going to want to grip a fork to eat or reach up to brush their teeth or wash their hair in the shower. They can be quite grumpy and perceived as resistant to care.

Sometimes with simple pain management, the elderly (or anyone) can regain the ability to care for themselves and get back to life.

Allowing themselves to just be daughters.

Bill's older brother came over to pick up Julia's older sister for a date on the beach the summer of 1946. Both sets of parents insisted they take along these two younger siblings. Bill and Julia fell in love that day. Not much could separate these two for the last sixty-six years.

Almost forty years ago Sally and Winter were set up on a blind date at a wedding in Napa, California. "One dance is all it took," Sally beamed. They were wed six months later. She found him to be an "incredibly romantic, lovely, wonderful person with unbelievable integrity and a hundred-watt smile; he was a dream."

In 2005, less than two years after Winter retired, their dream ended. He was diagnosed with Alzheimer's. He was fifty-eight. Caring for Winter became a twenty-four-hour a day job. Sally's health was deteriorating. How could anyone provide high quality care for a loved one with Alzheimer's, and for themselves, when they are physically and emotionally exhausted all the time?

Sally didn't realize how exhausted she was until her new 2012 car told her so. The drowsy driver alert system in her car insisted she was too tired to be on the road safely. This was her tipping point, along with the consequent urging of a close friend to take action. Sally felt that if she didn't make a change she would get seriously hurt, sick, or worse.

Sally then made the difficult decision to place Winter in a dementia facility. I think placement was the most loving course of action Sally could take for Winter, and for herself.

I asked her what advice she has for other people in the same situation. She urges people to take care of themselves by seeking the help of an Alzheimer's support group. Sally said, "I have become close friends with the people in my group. We care for one another, and I'm healthier for it. It's been an extremely important thing to do for myself. I don't feel alone in this."

The topic of life after death is a frequent subject of discussion and sometimes heated debate among family members and friends. When I am asked to participate in challenging spiritual or religious discussions, I speak in generic spiritual terms until I learn more about specific beliefs shared by the family. Even then I tread lightly with my words. I don't offer spiritual or religious advice, as we have chaplains whose role is to help families through tough questions of this nature. I typically try to stay present for the quandary, listen, and ask questions to possibly deepen or clarify the dying's own understanding.

If the tough conversations don't happen before the end of life, life can get really difficult in the end.

Rondelle suffered a stroke that left her alive enough to give her family the heartache of making decisions that Rondelle wouldn't have wanted. She had sufficient life left in her body, but not the quality kind. Her heart, kidneys, liver, and stomach were working adequately; her brain and lungs weren't. Rondelle didn't discuss her end-of-life choices with her family or have her wishes recorded. In a stressful moment, her family consented to a machine with a tube to breathe for her as well as a tube surgically placed in her abdomen to feed her. She was comatose.

If end-of-life decisions aren't made in advance, medical personnel legally have to take heroic measures to keep people alive. Family members are forced to make instant life and death medical decisions at a very stressful time. This is all too common. In this case, as a result, Rondelle suffered from crushed bones in her chest from CPR and her body was in an artificial prison for months. Even with the best round-the-clock care in intensive care units, comatose people like Rondelle still get bedsores, urinary tract infections, and pneumonias.

Have the tough conversation with your family, and put your wishes in writing. If you don't, what you want may not be honored.

Nancy and Marie were each near one hundred years old, sharp as tacks, and queen bees at their assisted living facility. Nancy spent most of her waking hours with her sweet sister Marie. They were goofy gals, constantly poking fun with loving banter. Nancy said goodbye to her each day, as if it were Marie's last. Nancy returned each day relieved and delighted that Marie was still with us. Marie said goodbye to her life every night before she fell asleep. She giggled in surprise to "wake up each day still alive."

We are told to practice saying goodbye as if it were the last time so we can live life to the fullest. What about the time between goodbyes?

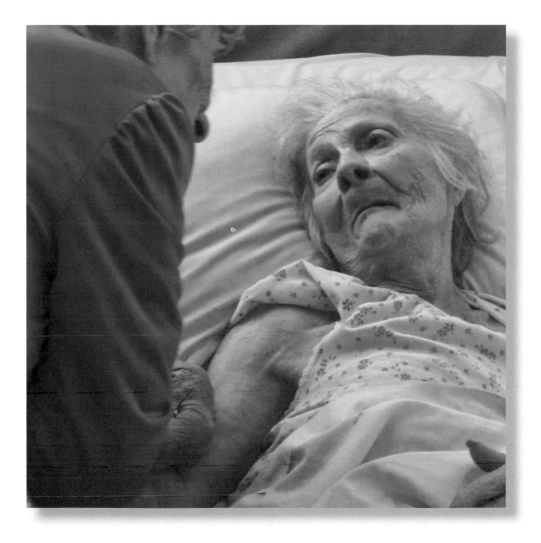

Is your family getting the best version of who you are? Or are they getting what's left after you have completed your to-do list?

Celebrate and love each other now. Let's not wait until we are dying to come together and openly love.

Paula tearfully whispered, "I'm dying in slow inches. I feel nailed to my bed." That's what Parkinson's disease does. It affects every aspect of life, very slowly. Physical independence is gradually lost. The disease itself isn't fatal. What is fatal are the complications of the disease: pneumonia, injuries related to falls, choking, an inability to swallow. Medications can prolong some quality of life—and extend the process of loss.

Paula was losing muscle tone all over her body. She was bedbound now, and her speech was difficult to understand unless you were a good lip reader. She grieved about not being able to talk with her grandchildren on the phone. She couldn't grip a pen to write letters anymore. Her mind remained sharper than most.

As I walked out the door of her tiny apartment, she waved me back to her bed and whispered, "If you knew you were dying and were allowed one phone call, who would you call?" Before I could answer her, she mouthed, "What are you waiting for?"

Unconditional Love

I've been present at enough deaths to know for sure that there is a great life force within us that is almost palpable when it leaves the body at the moment of death. I've been alive enough years to know that this human life can't be all there is. Many theories and belief systems cross my awareness about what happens next. Some make more sense to me than others. To me, it's a great mystery! There's not much I know with absolute certainty. Where this life force ends up, I'm not completely certain—yet.

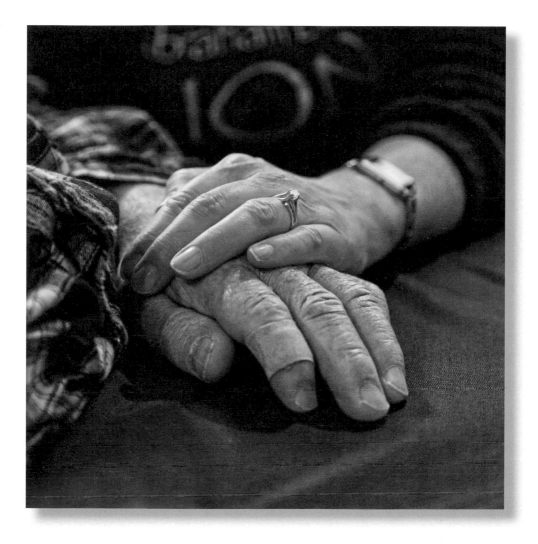

Over the years I have asked hospice patients to advise me on how to live my best life. Since they are facing death, their perspective on living shifts dramatically. I've received some pretty good advice.

Don't postpone happiness. Don't wait until the timing is right, when the kids are out of the house, when you have enough money, or when you are caught up. Live fully now. At any minute your life could change forever by disease or disability.

Stop watching TV and spend face-to-face time with the people you love. Don't assume they know how you feel. Leave your comfort zones and take risks for love. This is one of the significant regrets of the dying, that they can't go back and create happy, loving memories with the ones they are leaving behind.

Get out of the house. Play, be curious, take walks, appreciate nature, travel, dance. Dying people say they always had the intention to play, but never found the time.

Love, play, and be happy. Not bad advice.

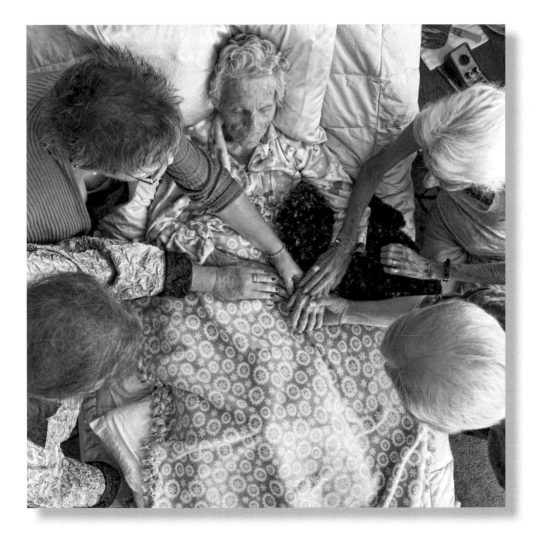

Acknowledgments

The inspiration for this book came from the stories and wisdom my hospice families have offered me over the years. I am in deep gratitude to the families who have given me permission to bring my camera into a most sacred and vulnerable time in their lives. I'm humbled by their generosity, and I'm honored and blessed to have crossed paths with them all. I have learned how to live by spending time with the dying.

Words can't begin to express my appreciation for my beautiful daughters, Sarah and Emily. These young women are my greatest teachers in the simple yet profound ways they love me. They keep me optimistic and hopeful for the future of this planet.

My dearest husband, Mark, has delivered me into a way of living and loving I didn't think was possible. He offers me an unwavering love and support that I wish for all.

I work with an incredible team of dedicated hospice workers who support me in more ways than they will ever know. Much gratitude to my hospice team in Medford, Oregon.

About the Author

Mary Landberg was inspired to go back to school at the age of forty-three to earn a nursing degree. Her plan was to work as a cardiac nurse and educator. One rotation in oncology, however, and she knew she had to work in end-of-life care. "I can't explain it, I instantly recognized caring for the dying as the truth of what I was supposed to do. I felt surprisingly comfortable with the death process." She soon became a certified hospice and palliative care nurse.

Hospice work gifts Mary with endless reminders of the value of selflessness and un-conditional love. Her faith in human connection is constantly renewed. This profession has helped Mary cope with the difficult times in her life. "I have grown rich in connections with my loved ones and have a deeper appreciation for my limited time here on this earth."

Mary Landberg MPH, is a hospice RN working in Southern Oregon.

Mary Landberg: Keynote Speaker

Author and award winning photographer Mary Landberg, MPH, is a hospice RN and advocate for hospice patients and families of the dying. Mary has profound insights to share based on participating in the care of hundreds of dying people. As a passionate speaker and dynamic storyteller, her engaging presentation style not only informs, but inspires, while exploring the sensitive and emotionally charged topics of death and dying.

Her presentation, *Conversations with the Dying…for the Living*, answers the question, "What is it like to die?" Mary provides an honest head to toe look at what occurs physically and emotionally in the last months, weeks, days, hours, and moments before death. Mary's unique experiences and reflections answer common questions and address emotional struggles patients and families face at the end of life.

Death is demystified. Audience members are encouraged to initiate those difficult yet important conversations about death and dying with family, friends, and clinicians for end of life planning.

Her simple yet powerful messages are delivered through poignant photographs and heartrending stories from her book, *Enduring Love—Inspiring Stories of Love and Wisdom at the End of Life*.

For more information please visit: www.enduringlovebook.com/speaking

Other Works and Collaborations by Mary Landberg

Mary Landberg's photographic adventures began just over five years ago with writing and self-publishing a book of photography and poetry, *Fear Means Go*, about the human condition. Mary wanted to capture the emotions in the poems with photographs of physical human expression in motion. She bought a camera and a remote shutter release, took photography classes, and began a three-year process of shooting self-portraits for the book. For excerpts from *Fear Means Go*, please visit www.enduringlovebook.com/books

Photography for the Uninhibited is another photographic adventure born from the *Fear Means Go* experience. Mary offers a dynamic portraiture service capturing the authentic spirit and passion of the fearless self. She provides people with a window into themselves and captures in photographs what people are most passionate about. View her portfolio at www.photographyfortheuninhibited.com

Mary is proud that one of her hospice portraits won first place in the National Hospice and Palliative Care Organization's creative arts contest. The NHPCO then featured her work in one of their articles, and soon other national publications helped spread the word. To view hospice portraits on line, please visit: www.hospiceportraits.com

Select photographs and stories from *Enduring Love*, *Fear Means Go*, and *Photography for the Uninhibited* are available to travel as an exhibit that invites people to live and love fully.

A portion of the proceeds from the sale of *Enduring Love* will support The Joy Boy Project, a community service collaboration with visionary nature photographer Mark Lunn. Many hospice patients die in beds that face blank walls. Mark decided to do something about that. He crafted a 39-inch by 26-inch nature collage with nine vibrant nature photographs, which he donates to hospice patients nationwide. His mission is to bring the beauty of nature to the walls and ceilings of the bedbound. For more information and to donate, please visit: www.enduringlovebook.com/joy-boy